T0120734

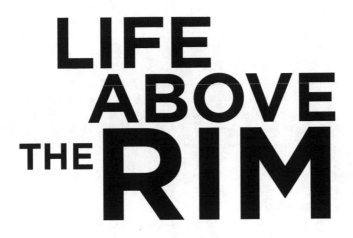

# LIFE ABOVE THE RIM

## TERRY CROWDER JR

WESTBOW
PRESS®
A DIVISION OF THOMAS NELSON
& ZONDERVAN

Copyright © 2021 Terry Crowder Jr.

All rights reserved. No part of this book may be used or reproduced by
any means, graphic, electronic, or mechanical, including photocopying,
recording, taping or by any information storage retrieval system
without the written permission of the author except in the case of
brief quotations embodied in critical articles and reviews.

This book is a work of non-fiction. Unless otherwise noted, the author
and the publisher make no explicit guarantees as to the accuracy of
the information contained in this book and in some cases, names of
people and places have been altered to protect their privacy.

WestBow Press books may be ordered through booksellers or by contacting:

WestBow Press
A Division of Thomas Nelson & Zondervan
1663 Liberty Drive
Bloomington, IN 47403
www.westbowpress.com
844-714-3454

Because of the dynamic nature of the Internet, any web addresses or
links contained in this book may have changed since publication and
may no longer be valid. The views expressed in this work are solely those
of the author and do not necessarily reflect the views of the publisher,
and the publisher hereby disclaims any responsibility for them.

Any people depicted in stock imagery provided by Getty Images are
models, and such images are being used for illustrative purposes only.
Certain stock imagery © Getty Images.

ISBN: 978-1-6642-2808-5 (sc)
ISBN: 978-1-6642-2807-8 (e)

Print information available on the last page.

WestBow Press rev. date:  04/05/2021

# DEDICATION

I would like to thank my support system that have all guided me with the best they had. I would first like to thank my mother who was a soldier in Christ for over three decades before she passed away on December 28, 2019. She showed how to love and endure the pain of not being loved back by those we care about most in life by the blood of Jesus Christ. Second my grandmother who has nurtured me from the very beginning and still is to this day and Gabrielle Gordon who has always been a supporter of my dreams and inspirations throughout the years. Third, I would like to thank my father for giving me mentorship about my responsibilities as a man of God. Last, I would like to thank all my family, friends and enemies. Love isn't a place nor a thing but god himself and to say I love anything or anyone I must recognize the source of love. I have relationship with God because of his love that he died for my sins on the cross. I am a sinner saved by grace and giving mercy to commit my life to Christ and be his living sacrifice in this temple he has giving me to love in and through. He built my support system of amazing and remarkable people who believed in me since infancy. To be able to write a book for the Most High is in itself and will always be a miracle of miracles. I am grateful and thankful for his sacrifice to allow me life in is very moment to write to you and have this conversation that is between friends. I hope this book helps you in this life to look for God in the chaos and confusion to find the peace and order you truly desire in your soul. I am just a saved messenger spreading the gospel of the Lord to those who may never pick up a bible but will pick of this book. My grandmother always stated that my life may be the only bible someone reads therefore I will with love take you to a *Life Above the Rim*.

# ACKNOWLEDGEMENT

I will like to thank God for allowing me the health to provide resources to support my book for his glory. I will like to also thank Gabrielle Gordon for her selfless contribution to my book for God's glory

# INTRODUCTION

This short novel is going to use basketball to bring to life an image of what it means to be Christian in today's world. I will express, illustrate and teach what the word of god wants you to know and the sport of basketball that connects with all races, religions, cultures and sex; will help me illustrate what the Holy Spirit has taught me. I will explain the truth of the gospel and eliminate the lies set by the world. and eliminate the grays of deceit set by cultural and world influences that in some way or another will deny you the choice to choose between truth of God and lies of today's culture no matter the place you live or language you speak. We can all relate on two things that we will have the privilege to experience. Those two topics are love and pain in which we are transformed by whether we choose to know or not. I'm here not to force or persuade anyone from what or who they believe in or believe of but I am here to state the truth of the gospel to reach those souls who are looking for hope, love, peace and healing by the holy power and nature of Elohim. Life Above the Rim is a term used in basketball to describe how a team or player plays if they are super athletic or fast. So, I took that saying or concept and made a spiritual compass to point you to our Savior and Lord, Jesus Christ! The rim is to represent the world and the rest is self-explanatory to explain where God is in our lives. He is above all situations, circumstances and problems of this world and the traps of the enemy who tries to keep you bound in sickness, depression, hate, pain and discouragement from tragedies that can harden the heart. The devil is a real enemy that is trying to take you out by any means necessary. Don't live in blindness anymore and choose to fight back the enemy at every corner and in every moment.

# PREFACE

This project started as a thought in my mind and I researched ways to write a book and get it published for free. I found an app called Wattpad and I have been writing ever since. The book gain more of my time and attention as I was guided by the Spirit to write more and more and more every day. I became so serious about this book and want connect with others in a way that doesn't require a screen to do just that. I share my happy and sad moments with you because of Christ. So when you pick up this book in your spare time remember it's all LOVE!

# 1

# PASSING IN FAITH

Let's talk my friend! I want to have genuine conversation with you throughout this short novel to help you reflect on your relationship with God and the content of your character. If you don't play any sport or play basketball you will be okay my friend. I will be with you throughout the short novel. Now let's begin in a situation that can change everything!

You are on the court with 10 seconds left to play and your team is down by a free throw. You have a good shot in the corner, but a teammate is open at the rim with a great shot in the post. What do you do?

A.  Shoot the 3
B.  Pass the Ball
C.  Call Timeout and Setup a play
D.  Freeze up / Turnover

What did you choose, yourself or your team?

That is a stressful moment to be in if you ever been in it. You have limited time and limited moves to win the game so what if F. happens or you missed the shot. How will you react to yourself with?

A. Anger
B. Optimism
C. Understanding
D. Frustration

Team success is always a sacrifice over individual play or stats. A lot of basketball players want to be that "guy ". What if being the" guy", cost you your success as well; by always "stuffing" the stat sheet to feed your ego. Every game can't be won by an individual alone as the greats have shown like A.I., Derrick Rose, LeBron James and Chris Paul or John Stockton gave up individual success for team success by passing the rock or the shine.

Same thing applies in life as well. You want to be the man or woman scoring with the ladies or guys stuffing your pockets and having everybody know who you are because it's your life. So, you feel entitled to be "the guy" or "that girl" in your life. How far does that get you watching out for you and your success. Something or someone around will suffer because of your idolatry of yourself. Your family will depend on you for something whether it's a dog all the way up to your wife or your husband or child.

Off the court you are still a part of a team and a team member has a role that she or he must flourish in as well for the team to have spiritual, mental and emotional success. Therefore, how can that happen if you only watching out for your needs, wants and desires? Your wife will need a pass, your children will need a pass, your husband will need a pass and other relatives will need a pass. Let me explain, see you are not passing a "basketball" around but you are passing your faith, love, commitment, time and attention around to your team. Unlike basketball where you will have a desire to defeat your enemy by the number of points you score but in life you have to pray for your enemies as well. The "basketball" that you are passing to your enemies is prayer with a sincere heart. You are the "basketball" or the" pass" to help your "team" or family score every day in life. To "score" in life is to help each other, those in need and those who hate you the most for any or no reason at all. Your actions matter, your words matter and your decision-making matters therefore, I will move on to my next point in being the "guy" or that" girl". Do you treat the poor or needy as your equal with such pride?! You seem to forget so easily that your life was a "pass" from Jesus Christ who gave you the ultimate "pass "of love by dying for your sins. He knows you will "score the bucket", because he has faith in who you are, and he ordained it that way. When you see that the "guy" of all the "guys" passing the rock for a good shot by faith in essence you will pass the rock again for a great "shot" to your fellow enemy, sister, brother or teammate. Sometimes you will miss a great shot or a good shot but doesn't make it any less of a great or a good shot. You are not perfect in any way! All Elohim asked us to do is love him, ourselves and our enemies with unconditional love no matter what. What happens if you miss the shot you can always catch the "rebound "and try again. A "rebound" in life is repentance and to forgive yourself and others for their mistakes against you. Prayer and forgiveness take effort much like a rebound in basketball. To get a rebound it takes timing, effort and grit when you want it bad enough it is already yours. How hungry are you for the love of God?

A. No appetite.
B. Maybe a bite.
C. I could eat.
D. I'm truly hungry!

How fast are you willingly to forgive your enemies and pray for them? Honesty is the key to true self-reflection.

A. I hold grudges
B. With a little time I will
C. Often but when I am ready
D. Immediately

If your answer wasn't immediately than you know that you have some work to do. Don't bash yourself or say anything negative about yourself. We have strength and weaknesses that we learn about ourselves throughout life. The answers to those weaknesses can only come from a walk with God. Day by day you are learning how to be more loving, forgiving and understanding of others to forgive them and move on with your life. There is compassion and peace in forgiveness that comes from the inside of your soul. Jesus forgave us by dying for our sins that holy day on Calvary which wasn't no easy feat to accomplish. We all have enemies or "haters" who try to belittle us or hurt us just because of who we are. Don't be ashamed of being wonderfully and beautifully made by the King of Kings. Do you love yourself unconditionally?

    A. I don't know
    B. Only when I'm in a relationship
    C. No
    D. Yes
    E. Sometimes
    F. Never

What did you choose Yes, Sometime or No? The truth is that your answer should always be a Yes! Yes! Yes! No matter if you are smiling or crying.

God loves you so much and never forget that he has you here for a purpose like no other my friend! You have to have faith that God will show you in due time.

What is wrong with waiting on God? You need time to grow and learn by being taught by God through the holy spirit

# REBOUNDING WITH COURAGE

Mistakes will happen on the court and off the court, but it isn't the misses or the mistakes that matters after you did but it's about how you are able to rebound, spiritually mentally, emotionally and physically once the shot is missed in life and on the court.

How do you respond to your mistakes?

A. Blame someone else
B. Take responsibility
C. Pray about it
D. You don't care either way

Do you think Kobe made every clutch shot in his career? No, he didn't, and he got laughed at for his misses in the game versus Utah early in his career because he air-balled it four times in the 1997 playoffs. Hard to believe Kobe missed clutch shots in overtime and got laughed at all in the same game.

Kobe didn't care he mentally rebounded back and won five NBA titles therefore he got the last "laugh "by continuing to be courageous and strong mentally and never losing faith! God will make your failures and shortcomings inspiration to inspire yourself or others. You don't have to be like anybody else when you are created wonderfully and fearfully by our Lord. So in life how do you rebound yourself when your ego bruised and your feelings are hurt?

A. Pray
B. Try to Ignore It
C. Blame others for the way you feel
D. Drug use (marijuana; etc.)
E. Get even /revenge

Yeah, you may get even on the court with a couple elbows and shoves to show that you are not a pushover. I knew you was a fighter but in life you have to forgive those who hurt you in any way to get that "rebound".

Believe me I understand, and I have done it in my playing days. I got a rebound off the rim and caught an elbow to the rib cage on the way down and the guy was 6'6 210. I am only 5'10 and 165 pounds soaking wet. His ego was bruised from little old 'me getting the rebound so he bruised me up with gravity and bone. I got up and dusted myself off physically and mentally and I focused on scoring and my defense the next few plays when he guarded me. I had to maintain my focus and not let my emotions dictate my thoughts nor my actions. I made three consecutive mid-range shots the next few plays to help my team. Do you know what the mid-range is?

A. The space between the post and the 3-point line.
B. I don't know

The mid-range is a jump shot that is between 10 to 15 feet from the basketball goal for you all that are new to basketball. The term "swimmer swipe" is a technique that smaller players use to deflect passes or steal the basketball from the bigger opposing player on the court in the post. God doesn't won't you to lose focus even when you are not in the wrong but back to the action.

Andddd we are back!!!

He took me to the post and every pass his teammate sent his way; I would do the "swimmer swipe" to get in front of the pass for a couple steals or deflections. He was bigger and stronger but I was hungrier and quicker than he would ever be. I refocused myself the same way when my mother died in December of 2019. Life was bigger and stronger than me in this situation after taking an elbow from "him "spiritually, I had to get that hunger, that aggression, and that focus back so I had to rebound my relationship with god. Rebuild the content of my character from the inside out in my adversity. Like I said before being the "guy" and taking the shot isn't always the best thing but when you miss ;God is always there to get the "rebound "to give you another "shot "at it. In my weakness I became the strongest me I ever been. Truly not because of my own merits and measure but God having mercy on me to make things right. You can't throw an elbow or a shove at life when there is nothing to hit at. Don't take things lightly when you are out there on the "court". God is with you therefore you know that "bucket "is going to go in but your work isn't done yet. Now, you have to get back on defense and what you are defending is more than your ego or image. You are defending your relationships, peace, love, livelihood, your enemies and your soul against the opposition and prayer is your defense. Keep your hands low, your eyes focused and your feet active because this team is crafty. You will have to use your spiritual smarts on this one. Don't let your emotions or negative words of others keep you from doing your best. Let's get it!

# 3

# DEFENSE IS DISCIPLINE

Defense isn't easy when you are moving through screens and watching for backdoor cuts on the baseline. This team is taller and bigger compared to your squad. Don't forget who got your back, yea that's right?!, God, Jesus and the Holy Spirit. So, zone it is on defense to protect the lane and make them work. The way the zone works is a defense set that put you in position to steal or deny the ball by trusting teammates to provide help defense. Therefore being on God's team you can't lose, and he already knows what they about to do. BASELINE! SCREEN! TRAP!, GO THERE!, I GOT YA MAN! is all communication and cooperation with the defensive anchor. See God is your best offensive player and defensive player as well, so you know he is working on the court. The enemy hits you with a hesitation move, in-out dribble with a crossover and drives to the basket from there I connect to his hip to hold my ground. He jumps into me and I move to avoid the foul(sin) and I got to trust God to bring help on the weak side. "SWAP!" and the ball goes flying in the other direction and the team is going the other way. The crowd is amazed at the block and the team chemistry to trust in each other. The other team isn't going to play fair and right. They are always going to try to play dirty and selfishly. God's team plays as a cohesive unit and the enemy plays in arrogance and pride but don't take them lightly because their mission is still the same. Dribbling in circles to make you reach in frustration and increase your anxiety to make you doubt or make a mistake. So, you have to stay calm and collected knowing God got your back even if you make a mistake. Every time you doubt your prayers or promises of God; the enemy will "score". What situations in your life cause you to doubt God?

A. Relationships
B. Money problems
C. Your environment
D. Social Media/ The culture
E. Your own heart / pride

The ball is back in your hands and now you have to get the ball to your best offensive player 92 feet away. It's time to break some ankles and get it to the best scorer. The holy spirit will give a seed to grow in yourself called self- control. Self-control is a spiritual discipline that helps you stay focused regardless of what is around. So, Let's Go! You got some work to do.

# 4

# DRIBBLE WITH PURPOSE

God trusts you with the "ball", so get moving point guard. Low dribble bent knees and controlling the game with your pace. One dribble, one move, and one step at a time and the enemy will try to make you react with swipes and pressure with every dribble. Stay calm and breathe into faith and having confidence in God; is having confidence in yourself. The other team wants what you got and that is your peace, joy, happiness, focus, compassion and your faith in God, therefore you got to guard that "ball "with your LIFE! Moves you practiced by yourself are flashing in your head like the scriptures in the Bible. You would practice until the moon came out is the same as praying until the sun came up when you are faced with new challenges. You remember how you trained, prayed and worked for this very moment. Have faith in what you learned and practiced with every dribble is in confidence. You get to half court and you notice a spiritual "trap" coming and you trust the moves God put in you. So, you quickly leave the enemy stunned by the quick in-out three day fast and a bounce pass of prayer to the corner into the hands of the "guy" on your team, Jesus Christ himself. Your work ethic didn't go unnoticed God got into position where you could see him to pass in faith all that you are and will be in him by sacrificing yourself for his glory. You were able to dribble with purpose because you believed in it and knew who to give it to! The same God you believe in will be believe you when he passes you the rock to "shoot".

What do you believe in?

    A. Just Yourself
    B. A you Purpose
    C. Nothing
    D. Faith in God

Dribbling with purpose is the same in life as walking in faith with God. You have to believe in yourself that you will keep the faith and continue to love God's people. Dribbling the ball so to speak; is just consistent prayer about all of your burdens and heartaches to God. You have to focused on your faith and not get distracted by fans praise and other team's slander. The devil wants to distract from what is eternal and put you in a place of lies and hopelessness. God is not a weak god in anyway or any form. We have limits and it has shown since the garden of Eden my friend. What is your truth? Do you truly believe in your divine purpose? Do you believe in the gifts, talents and or gifts God as given you? One of our gifts is to "dribble" with purpose and intention towards the other end of the court my friend.

# 5

# SHOOT WITH CONFIDENCE

God wants you to make "shots" in faith. The tough defense doesn't change the way you will shoot nor will "tough defense" in life will change what you believe. You are in the game and there is three seconds on the clock and Yah passes you the ball to shoot it for the "win" or gain victory in life over whatever struggles or sins that keep you away from him.

What are you going to do?

A. Pass the pressure
B. Shoot with Faith
C. Hesitate with Doubt

You should shoot in faith and never look back. God will allow things to happen in your life to see if you are truly faithful or playing faithful. It will always show on the court my friend!

Your destiny will be tested by the defense of doubt to shoot for your destiny and your dream. Yes as a man or woman it can be scary, intimidating or it leaves you vulnerable in some sense but do you let that stop you from taking the shot that God ordained for you to take it in victory!? It's a reason your hands are on that basketball (life). Your life includes all that you are and will be and isn't that worth every second in faith?! Shoot with intention to win in life by taking the shot of FAITH by trusting Yah completely. Take it with all of your strength, heart and soul because you have nothing to lose being where you are and everything to gain in turning away from your sins. It's cool to be the "man" or "woman" but in my opinion the sixth man is always part of the conversation like; Lou Williams, Jamal Crawford, Manu Ginobli, and Isaiah Thomas to name a few; who played their roles into greatness by being humble and letting the "star" do the rest. In my life I have always tried to choose or say what is best for me regardless of the situation. The world tells you; "You Can Be Whoever You Want To BE!" but that mindset can hinder you. That mindset hinders you because it cuts Yah out of your life. Shooting in confidence is from preparation of long hours of doubt, fustration and reptition. You are training diligently for that big moment that could change your life!

So let me ask you what are you training for?

    A.  A Dream
    B.  Money/ Fame
    C.  Family
    D.  Ego

Who is training you?

    A.  Yah (God)
    B.  Your own judgement

What do you consider that "MOMENT"?

    A.  Going pro
    B.  Recongition
    C.  Relationship/Marriage/Having a Baby
    D.  Being Successful(Finanically)

Where is Yah in your decision-making?

    A.   some of my decisions
    B.   none of my decisions
    C.   all of my decisions

There are moments in our lives that we desire to be our best in and we do our best to prepare in advance for those moments. I can say that I haven't always made good decisions because the way I prepared did not include Yah at all. To be my very best is this life; I must acknowledge that my best may not be enough. That is where Elohim can now train me with the correct preparation for those moments. My confidence changes dramatically when I acknowledge my pride and recieve instruction on my "shooting form". Now I am making godly decisions. Jehovah is my counselor, trainer, coach and discplinary when it comes to what I say and what I do. He loves me enough to care about my daily life but is also the reason I can have those decisions. I am shooting with confidence no matter what situations appear in my life because I remember who help me prepare in advance. Shoot with Confidence!

# 6

# NOTHING LIKE LOU

Sixth man of the year is an award I always dreamed about holding up one day. I never was looking to be the "star "or have scoring titles but to hold up that Sixth Man trophy 🏆 is my dream. What comes with the sixth man award is sacrifice, endurance, humility, hope and flare in your role and being apart something bigger than yourself. Dropping who you were before for something more and greater. In comparison it's the same way as being saved and walking with god in faith. You are the sixth man who sacrifice your flesh to walk in the spirit with Jehovah. A sixth man is good at few things but mostly "scoring "on a team during tough games to get the win. The best thing a follower of Yahweh does on his team is pray in faith to him for everything is like "scoring "a bucket through tough situations or tough defense on the court. You move in a way that is still you, but you don't belong to you anymore but God's will and the holy spirit. Serving yourself doesn't bring joy or peace in your life for long. When you allow yourself to be an instrument of Elohim's you will begin to change people's lives for the better and that's worth being God's Sixth Man for eternity.

What is your "playing "status with God spiritually?

A. Day to Day
B. Questionable
C. Injured
D. Out for Season

# 7

# COACHING IS LOVE

Don't act like you knew how to dribble or shoot as a kid growing up. Some of y'all were lucky to have a father figure or father around you to show you the game. I wasn't one of the lucky ones, but it didn't mean I couldn't coach myself how to play. God saw my passion for the game in my heart. I didn't realize every time I prayed before I practiced God became my coach. I would sneak in the old gym at Bolton High School after getting cut from tryouts my sophomore through senior years to get in a couple more repetitions. My couple repetitions turned into couple of hours of being at school after 2 'o clock and staying until four with my "coach". Just me, God, the court, the ball and some old chairs dribbling and shooting. After every shot I made or move I started to use naturally over time in my head I got a "good job "or I would high five gesture myself. I just love God and the game of basketball became my way of worship and praise after school, work, or during my semi-pro practices. I would be so at peace until I would entertain negativity from other teammates, the coach, or bystanders. God was coaching me how to be within myself with him and nothing else would matter. Therefore, when I lost my relationship with him my game changed or became non-existent because I wasn't enjoying the game anymore because he wasn't there to coach me or cheer me on. I was okay not having a dad or support of my dream, but I did have a heavenly father who supported my heart and soul. Coaching is important from God because he teaches you how and what to say and do; however sometimes you not doing much at all but listening to what he has to say. I wasn't arrogant by any means but like all relationships being a "child" spiritually I got tired of not having what I thought God would give me through my sweat from the hills I ran or the tears of frustration when I couldn't get that move right. Putting expectations on him in my life collapsed our relationship. He answered me with a lesson one day after semi-pro practice when I got into an altercation with a fellow teammate who was choosing to do the wrong thing and I made a choice to do the wrong thing by leaning on own my understanding and I made a big mistake. By losing my relationship with God it cost my ability to play for a while because of an injury caused by a titanium bat smashing against both shin bones in my left leg. He sat me down to where I had to listen again and get myself right with him. I was hurt until I realized that he was coaching me to open my spiritual eyes. God's coaching is of a father and a father will discipline you in love to help you grow or turn back to him. Coaching is his word, his love, his patience, his compassion and his commitment to you from the very beginning and sometimes he will help you remember that through trials and tribulations.

How do you see being benched in life?

    A. A learning experience
    B. Humbling experience
    C. Lame, God doesn't know what he is doing!
    D. A and B

It's okay to be angry but sin is not a commandment in Ephesians that shows you how to respond, reflect and apply what you learn to your life. The most important reason coaching from God is worth the hurt, the pain and the discipline is because he loves you. However, you respond is your choice alone as a person therefore who do you choose God or yourself?

# 8

# LIFE BEYOND LIMITS

What can you do when you fail at something; after giving your ALL to that craft or situation?

A.  Keep trying
B.  Listen for God

Some people continue trying and some choose to take a step back from pursuing your dreams to acknowledge God. A dreamer is the most powerful person in the universe. To have a dream that scares you out of your mind and take hold of all your focus when you wake is a gift that we all received but some lose hope and others are still dreaming of that one day things will be better or even to some perfect. The dream comes to life by your actions to grow that dream to its greatness potential. God doesn't give you false hope to have a dream. He gives you real hope for a real dream that hasn't become reality just yet.

Have you ever prepared for something over and over again until you grew sick of it? Breaking those previous limits that you had before and pushing you to a new level that you can't see with your physical eyes. How can the very thing that makes you sick, be turned into something that cures you from all your anxiety, worries and discouraging moments?

That's the true power of God when you really self-reflect on how far you come. You learn true faith when you in a place that's beyond your limits. You see how far you come in reading this book? It seems as though we know each other far better than before.

# 9

# SMILE FOR THE FANS

James Ch 1. v 2 is what we all are living at this very moment. Take a few moments to read that scripture and meet me back here! So, let's continue on with our conversation shall we my friend.

It's hard sometimes to smile in life especially when you are faced with adversity and hardships. It is hard to smile when those who you thought would be there to the end change into an enemy or a complete stranger. It seems like life is an ocean and waves are the people you once cherished but now you have to be careful not to drown in the sadness of it all. When you are able to smile in those times, it can inspire you to be genuinely happy and optimistic about any situation. You will hear more negative words than positive in any sport you will play or that dream you are currently pursuing. When the heart smiles it does something to you soul that enlarged the colors, food and the people around you into complete prosperity and joy that the world couldn't understand it or even grasp.

How do you respond to name-calling or trash talk?

    A. Respond back
    B. Smile
    C. Ignore it

You are not weak for ignoring harsh words or actions. You are not weak for returning kindness for wickedness. You are not weak for smiling at those who would rather watch you fail with extra popcorn instead cheering you on to succeed in life specifically in that sport or that dream that you are pursuing consistently and diligently with all your heart, soul and mind. People are meant to change but they choose whether for the better or for the worse. Those who choose for the better continue to love life as it is regardless of how painful or misconstrued it can become. So, what makes you smile?

A. God
B. Job / Position
C. Your dream
D. Family
E. Friends
F. Hobbies
G. Relationship
H. All the Above

Everyone has someone or something in their life that makes them smile on the inside more than anything else in life. For some it is temporary things and for other it's an eternal purpose in God. You have start somewhere with something or nothing grows inside. Nothing can grow in the snow and ice of a harden heart or broken soul. We all can appreciate such moments of happiness and everything that is going right and well in our lives, but I have come to appreciate the bad, the ugly and the downright painful moments in life by gaining joy from my relationship with Jesus Christ. The inspiration to love it all through thick and thin is truly worth smiling about even when nobody seems to care or wander about how you are feeling or doing.

# 10

# VAIN GLORY MVP

People don't love what you have or your accolades that you gain over time. People love who you are and will see you has inspiration in their own lives to achieve greatness. No matter what you gain it's all vain glory not because people praise you for remaining focused or determined but because when you leave this world people won't remember what you do or who you know but how you made them feel in the end. They felt cherished, admired, appreciated and loved by you in some form or fashion tailored specifically for them. You may have said something nice or encouraging to a complete stranger or strangers who to take that seed of hope and grew into a new relationship, job or life. You never know who you could inspire to be more than who they are now. The little things that make up your character is what can be inspiration or humiliation; don't be the second option for vain glory of being on a different level than anyone else. People don't care if you are rich, well-spoken or dress well; it's how you use your god given opportunities and gifts when you interact with people in daily life. When you search for true humility in your weaknesses you tend to find truth that is more precious than god or diamonds. It's the truth that lives and breathes as you do. He understands who you are down to the very atom of your being in due time when you realize how greatly detailed life is; you will take a moment to realize how much your words and actions matter to individuals or that one individual. Don't get so caught up in grasping at vain glory of fame and riches with a "told you so" demeanor as if you weren't sleeping in your car or buying ramen noodle packets for lunch while living in a college dorm. People always change for something or someone but why change for vain glory that has no power or influence to change lives of the many with just a simple kind gesture towards someone who may recycle that moment in time again and again. That kindness may turn into walking an elderly lady across the road or a homeless man feeding the birds with probably his only meal today, but you were able to provide that service by the mercy and grace of God. You may be the only bible someone will read in their entire life. Let your life be more than choices of vanity and selfishness. Be the light that is brighter than sun for someone who had rainy days. Your kind words and actions of love can inspire someone to endure. Vain glory is like a gift that you knew nothing about until you unwrap it and you realize that excitement of imagining what was in the box was more of a gift than the actual gift that was in the box.

What would be a gift that would make you prideful?

A.  Money
B.  Rolex
C.  Brand new exotic car
D.  Brand new mansion

Vain glory will provide all you could have imagined but yet your dream was the gift from the beginning and not the things that eventually came with it from your success. Anytime you watch an interview of an influencer, athletes or celebrities being acknowledged by fellow peers and fans for what do they exceptional well is to acknowledge your passion or love you put into your craft. Those extraordinary people don't have excitement for those accolades or awards they may receive but they tend to light up about being able to provide for more than themselves in the need and wants. The fame nor fortune isn't worth as much as putting a smile on someone's face that truly cherish and love.

It may seem like that's the greatest fulfillment of the soul to have and to give abundantly without a care in the world.

If you didn't have to work ever again, what would you be doing right now?

    A.  spending time with family
    B.  find other ways to work
    C.  travel
    D.  be a lazy couch potato

That's why some people play the lottery because they believe more in that chance of winning than they believe in their god given talent or talents. How strange is that to believe in a system that gives you the slim chance to win and live how you want to. When I am at the gas station paying for gas, I always see someone chasing that dream of striking it rich for a small fortune. I tried once and decided that it wasn't a dream worth chasing in the end. Your humility can be truly appreciated when you work for your wealth instead of putting on a game of chance. Poverty tends to make your ultimate goal or dream about money and not about spiritual prosperity in the long run because you only see with your physical eyes. From that point you only see satisfaction in having money of some kind on your body or in your possession.

How much would you spend on jewelry?

    A.  0- 9k
    B.  10 k - 40 k
    C.  50 k - 100k
    D.  100k - 500 k +

Culture of the world tends to place the value of something on how much you paid for it. Rappers buy chains for glory of image and a marriage proposal composed of diamond rings or ring. How much do you think your soul worth?

A. Priceless
B. Priceless!
C. Priceless!!
D. Priceless!!!

Your soul is priceless because a price was paid by Jesus in blood. The truest act of love and sacrifice to give sinners like you and me a true chance at real peace and prosperity. Vain glory is lust of the eyes and you will never be satisfied in what you have because at some point the magnifying glass will be focused on you and humility will not be the content of your character because your dream can be caught in the nets of vain glory.

# 11

# TEAM M VS TEAM R/P

Marriage is the covenant honored before God and joined by him as it is stated in Matthew 19:6.

How do you view marriage my friend?

    A.  Something to do
    B.  A way to satisfy Companionship
    C.  Holy
    D.  A commitment to your true love
    E.  B, C, D
    F.  I don't believe in marriage

I see and where did you get your point of view on marriage from? –

    A.  Movies
    B.  Books
    C.  Personal experience
    D.  Mom or Dad

Do you believe those sources of reference about marriage shaped the way you choose your relationships?

A. Yes
B. No

Did you see a form of intimacy outside of conversation and quality time spent with a person such as kissing, cuddling or sexual display in some way?

A. Yes
B. No

Do you believe your relationship(s)you were in or are currently in:

A. sexually driven
B. spiritually driven
C. emotionally driven?

When you answer these questions it just conversation between friends. I want you to see where parts of your life may be transparent and other parts of your life covered by dust of confusion and sin. From my own personal experience in a relationship with God; areas in my life that were dirty and dusty became transparent like glass from the heat of the Holy Spirit putting things in black and white. Destroying all the grays of instant gratification and emotional stimulation. A lot of couples show how wonderful and exciting their relationship is on social media with matching outfits, cars, and demeanors to the world which in turn others would want to have or be like them in some way, form or fashion. Is that the real truth of a real relationship or am I to cover a sex driven or emotional driven partnership between two souls? I believe we all are to meet that one that God has for us someday, but our pursuit of our own desires could destroy all that God has for us including the marriage we are supposed to have between God, your wife and your husband. If you don't believe in marriage as being the standard for everyone then that is what you believe however doesn't mean it is true.

A. Yes a partnership
B. No a relationship
C. Maybe I don't know

God allows us to choose where we go, who we meet and what we say because real love doesn't force a way of life or relationship on anyone. Without god in a "relationship "between husband and wife, it then becomes a partnership of give and take. Those partnerships are form from sex, emotional connection and words of compassion. Aren't we missing something here? Where is God in all of this? He isn't "in "there to begin with and he won't be there when it ends. God will always be there for you because he loves you but shacking, dating, casual sex nor Netflix and chill are holy to God. God honors the holiness of marriage stated in Ephesians 5:25 and not what society has adopted. People blame God for their choices after a heartbreak or betrayal. When truly in the beginning God wasn't acknowledged at all about that person you decided to choose. The world culture is pushing the boyfriend and girlfriend titles as legitimate based on that fact that both parties act as though they were married to each other. If that was true, why does a person find another girlfriend or boyfriend as time goes on? How can something that is respected as permanent be so fragile and temporary once things change. To brag and boast about what he or she received on Valentine's Day or their birthday to show the "status "of their partnership. The culture has turned what is supposed to be enjoyable between God, husband and wife into advertising for others to marvel and compare to.

Do you believe that you place your expectations on your significant other from what you see on social media or from celebrities couples?

A. Yes
B. No

Expectations on how that person should be or respond isn't love but more of manipulation of what looks good to your eyes. Do you see a person for who they are or who they can be to you?

    A. Yes, I see them for who they are
    B. No, I see who they can be in my life
    C. Neither

The source behind what a person does or choose to say is very important. The source of this book is love and is inspired by love to plant seeds of love between friends.

There can be antagonist or a protagonist as the source behind your expectations and choices. Is God guiding your choices or is it your own lustful desires?

    A. God
    B. It's my life, I choose
    C. I don't know
    D. Never thought about it like that.

## 12

# PAIN ISN'T A INJURY

How do you view pain in your life?

    A.  Necessity
    B.  A disease
    C.  Neither there nor here
    D.  Punishment from God

Where do you go for comfort?

    A.  God
    B.  Porn
    C.  Drugs/ Alcohol
    D.  Short term sexual partners /relationships

We all have experienced some form of pain in different events of our lives. The issue of mindset can either help you or slowly break you down. Pain is something you cannot avoid whether you are rich or poor. Why do you think that is? Pain wasn't an invention of God it was a result of our sinful nature that accompanied it. It was introduce long before you and I was even thought of. Adam made a choice whether we agree with it or not; his choice was sin over God. Nobody knows what tomorrow will bring but it will soon be a yesterday far from the echo of your steps. The years have been gliding gently; leaving a mark of time on your skin that doesn't describe how much you endured or had to push through. Those wrinkles and touches of gray just show that you have been here awhile, and you have gotten stronger with every touch. You don't have to be middle-aged or old to experience traumatic experiences in life. I have meet some of the most amazing people who went through a lot at young age but are not defined by those events at while still in their youth. Take away the drugs, alcohol and the sex or porn to be a painkiller to your life; how do you cope now? I'm not saying people don't choose healthy ways of coping with life tragedies but that's a small population compared to those who choose those negative means to distract their mind from being consumed by their volcano of emotions. Erupting with tears of agony and regret about what could have been different or still the same. Letting go of the pain will expose either your extreme anger or extreme fear or sometimes even both when you are trying to filter out all the lava that has been compressed for years.

What has been a painful experience for you?

    A.  Lost loved one
    B.  Job Loss
    C.  Breakup
    D.  Abuse (sexual, verbal, emotional)

You thought your pain made you stronger as you gotten older but really you can't feel anything. You are so numb that ice would catch hypothermia from your cold soul. To say you are tired of feeling is to poke at you are tired of living in the best parts of your life. I have been in more fights, arguments and uncomfortable situations than I can count but it is still my life to live. God has always tried to guide me I the direction of holiness and peace. I was the one who chose to have sex, smoke weed, fight, gamble and live life how I see fit. I did go to the military to get discipline but really it was God getting me alone to talk with me and help me understand all of it was vanity. He came through a gentle soul by the name of SPC Bennett and we would read the bible and pray together throughout boot camp especially when we were in the cold and wet mud of the Missouri hills. People quit long before they are shark attack outside the barracks. God has always been my best friend even when I didn't want him around or ignore his whispers. I was so wrong and childish in a lot of ways because I left my first love.

I have noticed with a person becoming "numb "they tend to want to escape to something that gives them a "good" feeling about being alive or just being able to feel altogether. You have to see that pain isn't a disease but a necessary part of our character development. God used our bad and turned it to good every single day far beyond our understanding of how things should work based on our own personal experiences, feelings and views. In our spirit we know that there is more but our we patient enough to go through the process of being cultivated and reinvented to be in that place of more than enough. The part of me that last forever however I cannot not see with my eyes but the part me that I can see has a limited amount of time to breathe, talk, walk and live! Why embrace a mindset that focus on being numb and narcissistic or pessimistic towards life or everyone I meet? Is that the life our god would want us to live and maintain? Do you think God would want a mindset like that in his presence or in heaven? Do you see more than with your senses? What do you truly believe?

The deeper our trust grows throughout this conversation I come to learn that we aren't so different after all. We may perceive things differently than each other but we can feel the same. Pain makes us sad, angry or discouraged most of time but what happens if you take from pain... joy! Yes, I said joy that can't be explain by your senses or your thoughts. Spiritual joy is in your pain like a seed buried in the ground. You can't see it nor can you feel it growing but nonetheless it is growing every moment. Take that seed and plant it in the fertile ground of God spirit and watch the impossible, the unexplainable and the unimaginable happen.

Psalm 18 v 2
The Lord is my rock, and my fortress and my deliverer; my God, my strength, in whom I will trust ;my buckled, and the horn of my salvation, and my high tower.

# 13

# LEGACY

Legacy is a word that everybody understands but some lack consistent discipline to reach it. Your legacy is what you chose your life to be about in its' content. In the bible it tells the lives of those who's legacies are exalted in name of Jesus Christ. Great rulers like Joseph and Daniel stayed loyal to God even though they were wealthy. A legacy of being obedient to the Almighty and his people will always build your legacy brick by brick. I understand that having a legacy doesn't mean you need to be rich or famous to be recognized or valued by others. Just being who God created you to be is the legacy in a lane of its' own. Nobody can ever say what you say or do what you do.

What will be your legacy?

- A. You don't know
- B. You don't care
- C. God (Love)
- D. Fame and Fortune

This conversation is strictly between us and God. The roots will always tell you how much potential a tree has but have you ever heard a tree complain about growing or bad weather? The tree roots grow deeper and deeper. It focus is on enduring, growing and changing. It is not design to worry about the storms. We don't have roots or branches, but we do have families, friends and enemies all around us. To love god is to love yourself and to love his people unconditionally regardless of the offense or wrongdoing. It is always the closest ones to you that cause the most harm. Isn't the hurt the same regardless of the face that you identify it with? We all truly believe and desire to be loved and to love but sin open the door to hate, murder and chaos not God. I would want my legacy to be one that honors God and not man in anyway. Just really think about it for a moment and realize you get to pray to Creator of the Universe! It's not about how rich, famous or smart you are that you get this opportunity every day but it's because he loves you with a every lasting love far beyond our understanding of what love truly is. The bible says that love is God and it never fails! NEVER! So, wouldn't you want a legacy that exalts such a God and purpose? I'm not here to make you a christian but this conversation is to show you the love of God and I come as friend in Christ. You may not remember what I said but you will remember how I made you feel and truly I hope you felt loved throughout this conversation that we have had in this short novel. Like I said before, this conversation between friends talking about everything together. Just remember when all I responsible for our own conduct towards ourselves and God's people; to be specific, our people. Love is the only legacy that endures forever because love will always be and is forever the Highest all-powerful GOD! That will be who my legacy exalts.

What do you want your legacy to be in the end? Explain in the detail.

# GOD'S DRAFT PICK

You ever been the last to be pick for mostly everything growing up. I have whether it was basketball, kickball, tag, hide and seek or flag football. It didn't really matter if I was first or last because a person's position doesn't make or break them in the long run of things. The most important time in your life where position was the most important was when you were conceived. You were picked by God out of 400 trillion other sperm cells! The creator picked you as his number one draft pick into the world and yet we value man's status of us more than him! You may never be drafted by the NBA, MBL, NFL, or NHL in the near future but in this present moment you are number one of one to God. Jeremiah Ch 1 v 5 states he knew you before you were conceived in your mother's womb. You don't have to be a top athlete, artist, or etc. in the world to be known. You are known by the one who created the world! I just try to imagine how I looked before I was a sperm cell sometimes friend and yet I can fathom it at all. When you are told something negative about how you look or sound, speak Jeremiah Ch 1 v 5 in your spirit and let those naysayers know that they are loved and known by the same God who made you.

Why do we value the opinions of others so much?

A. I don't know
B. It's because we all want to be accepted

C. It's lonely being different

D. None above

Naysayers could be strangers or closed love ones that have opinions we value because we love them, but we shouldn't value them more than God's opinion of us. Those negative opinion are like seeds that grow low self-esteem, depression, and lack of self-love in the depths of our very soul. It takes away the fire in us to enjoy life and God's people. The enemy only comes to steal, kill and destroy who you are! Don't do the job for him by allowing negative opinions of others derail yourself love. Accolades, awards and to be recognize for what you can do is nice but not as fulfilling as being able to acknowledge someone for their talent or uniqueness by being their self. To exist in a space of complete peace is one of the greatest rewards you are given by the goodness of God.

What do you love most about yourself?

A. Your soul (God)

B. Love for people

C. Your physique

D. Your personality

E. Your attitude

Continue to cherish who you are and what you love to do. You are wonderfully and fearfully made by God who knows the hairs on your head. Never forget you are God's number one draft pick. He chose you for a loving purpose that includes all your flaws and short-comings. The questions that we have can be answered but only if we are ready to listen and just hear what God has to say. To take in account how you are created with intelligence and creativity that sin has kept dormant and you from being called upon the greatest stage in the universe which is the throne room of God Almighty.

THE END

# EPILOGUE

This short novel is just one of the many examples of God's nature in every way because he will take an idea and bring it to life without said a word to express his love for all of us. I never imagined writing a book for people to read and allow it to counsel them in such a way that is thoughtful, compassionate, real, vibrant and humble to all who will encounter it. This was so supposed to be conversation between me and God that allow nomadic streamers to take a walk through its entirety based on my very own personal relationship with him. I believe this book will bring you closer to seeing God for who he truly is and not what the world or culture try to portray an image of evolution or science as the Creator of us and all that is living. Our spirits know more than we do by far and tat is why we choose to persevere through it all. You are a creation that knows how to be, how to think, how to feel, how to move, and how to create art, music, technology, food and the list continues on and on. The conversation that expands beyond the impeccable point of companionship, conversation, truth and understanding that seems like we are on the tip of the iceberg of our spirituality. We all desire infinite life that is full of happiness peace, selfless and true love. God has made a book that can talk back and love you where you are at. I take zero credit for this impossible feat from my perspective can only be delivered from Elohim himself.

# ABOUT THE AUTHOR

Terry Crowder Jr was born in the year of 1996 to the beautiful couple in Alabama. He grew up playing with animals and loving the outdoors. A bubbly child that said hello in a way that tickle the souls of anyone who came in touch with him. He loves life and traveling so he joined the U.S. Army to see all that he could see. After leaving the military and coming back home to his Mississippi roots; then decided to see the U.S. through the trucking industry. The beautiful cities of Baltimore and Philadelphia were his favorite and smell of the ocean breeze shivered his soul. He always loves good food, people and music from all cultures. The city of New Orleans had some good gumbo and grits in the morning in the days he spent in Gulf. He loves God, his self, his family and his enemies without shame. He continues to see color in life no matter the troubles and circumstances. He is a saved man and continues to keep the faith and remain obedient to his Almighty Lord, Jesus Christ.

Printed in the United States
by Baker & Taylor Publisher Services